Odd Corners
in Appleby

Gareth Hayes

HAYLOFT

First published 2002

Hayloft Publishing, Kirkby Stephen,
Cumbria, CA17 4EU.

tel: (017683) 42300
fax. (017683) 41568
e-mail: dawn@hayloft.org.uk
web: www.hayloft.org.uk

ISBN 1 904524 00 1

A catalogue record for this book is available
from the British Library

Cover illustration: *Appleby Horse Fair, Rosemary Morison*
All photographs by the author unless otherwise stated.

Produced in Great Britain
Printed and bound in Hungary

To my children,

Amos Stanley Hugh and Millicent Friday

Protecting the Future by Preserving the Past.

This work of co-ordination automatically produces an aesthetic. But an aesthetic unattached to a general philosophy is, if not absurd, at least incomplete. I have reversed, in order of conception, the usual method. I have proceeded from aesthetic to a philosophy, instead of finding place in a philosophy for an aesthetic.

Vernon Blake,
Relation in Art – being a suggested scheme of art criticism,
Oxford University Press, 1925

CONTENTS

ILLUSTRATIONS

ACKNOWLEDGMENTS

I cannot sing the praise loud enough of the folk who have, and continue to, motivate me in my modest ambitions. Particular attention should be paid to Catherine and Beryl at Appleby Library, the ladies of Appleby Business Service, and the staff at Penrith Library (even though it is in Cumberland). Thanks also go to John T. Hall and Mary George for their help with some of the illustrations. And finally to Sowerby and Jones who continue to make me smile.

INSPIRATION

Aesthetic value can be found in anything close to the heart. It is the nature of our being that what is beautiful is common in the images that we derive from nature itself. From this standing we must also consider man-made structures. Digging deeper we can add man-made structures that relate a story of our inner being, of our struggle towards survival, mixing past with present and communication with continuity.

Whether it is an antique shop or a sports arena, a post-box or a sign-post, a simple road or a complex roof, there will be a rewarding picture for everyone.

The imagery becomes clouded when considering not only the bigger picture, like a whole town, but also the people within. The mist clears when accepting the Appleby aesthetic. To the frequent visitor, the passing traveller and indeed the town's locals, the many touristically inclined shops in Appleby will only stock post-cards and memorabilia dedicated to the five major features of this historic market town - the wide street of

Boroughgate with the Moot Hall island and sanctuary of St. Lawrence's Church; the defending Castle and towering Norman Keep; the tree-lined River Eden viewed from the town's main bridge; the bridge itself, most commonly taken as gypsy horses wade deep in the river at New Fair time; and Appleby Railway Station, oft winning awards for the best kept and the friendliest station on the famous Settle to Carlisle railway line.

Whilst justifying their place in Appleby's portfolio of timeless tradition, there is much more to the town. Many more places to see and enjoy. Inevitably the tides of percentages draw the subject matter to railways, religion and Romany. It is only right to pay due respect to their relevance. Yet my intention is to highlight a few interesting and unique corners to be found on both sides of the looping River Eden as it protects and nourishes the townsfolk with its own commanding odd corner.

My observations are inspired by travel writer William T. Palmer. Palmer began writing a series of themed books as early as 1902, but really came into his own with his walking diaries of the 1930s. One of his early works on landscape and life was entitled *Tramping in Lakeland*. Now highly collectable, it may not have received the praise it deserved, perhaps because of the ambiguous title. In 1936 Palmer issued *Odd Corners in English Lakeland* and a year later was able to issue a sequel, appropriately called *More Odd Corners in English Lakeland*.

Palmer's passion for fell and dale was matched by his skills as a writer. His countryside explorations also brought us Odd Corners in North Wales, the Yorkshire Dales, Derbyshire and even Surrey. With a slight change of tack, tackle and tiring limbs his later books were prefixed as "Wanderings in", but not before he spread the net of original hikes to add a "Verge of" series to his most favourite regions. Sadly, although neighbouring his beloved Lakeland, he was not a frequent visitor to the Eden Valley and descriptions of the area were minimal. I honour him by quoting from his short piece about Appleby in *The Verge of Lakeland*, before completing the jigsaw and giving my own version of *Odd Corners in Appleby*:

In my school class I was taught that in the Middle Ages, Appleby was the third or fourth largest town in northern England, after York and Newcastle-on-Tyne or Durham, but that war and plague had destroyed most of its importance. When I tramped into it through Scattergate past the Doomgate and Castle gate, I was thrilled. I found a pretty quiet little community, busily minding its own affairs, and with no eyes for a strange, wondering lad. There were no scattered ruins, no skeleton of a town, not even walls or enclosures. I walked over the River Eden bridge, then with its ends square packed with small houses, shops and inns, looked at the Assize Court on The Sands, heard the chime of a clock, and made off at my best pace past Burrells over Orton Scar and home again...

To the hurrying motor-tourist, Appleby is too often a stage name - so many miles from - somewhere else. The main road keeps east of the Eden and by-passes the town though the church is seen across a stretch of river, and the castle, with ancient keep and modern-times residence, is visible on the sandstone bluff. The pretty

Boroughgate extends from the Cloisters outside the churchyard up a steep incline to the gate of the castle grounds; it is easy to make a side tour into the town, and to admire its beauties, but few cars pause to do so. The vehicles parked in the open space have usually local number plates, farmers and other people shopping in the town.

According to critics Appleby was ever sleepy, yet ever on the point of wakening up. But faith in the awakening was badly tested when first a branch railway, then a main line came along the Eden Valley to serve the town. It would seem that Appleby's "active people" merely drifted to Penrith or Carlisle, or to Yorkshire. They did not secure return tickets, and so the town went back to its sleep. And the motor buses serve pleasure rather than profit. It would be unfair, however, to leave the impression that the old county town is lazy and feckless, a place living on its capital and ancient fame, doing nothing for itself. The people are content to look after their own affairs. There is good business, and a fair social life...

The future of Appleby - I'm no prophet, but it is situated in the centre of some of the finest farms in Britain, and its importance should not lessen. The great Express Dairy undertaking means that milk is collected and handled locally, and provides some permanent employment. For the rest, Appleby is not badly situated, though the parcel post and cheap sales in cities may reduce the scope and stock of some of the shops. And of course the specialisation of multiple shops has some effect on the outlook. However, I believe and trust that Appleby will remain, on the surface and below, as carefree as it has been in the past.[1]

Appleby, perhaps surprisingly, is a good place to be alone; to be thoughtful in the pleasure of one's own company. It is also a fine place to be in the company of others. My personal needs are gratified by a combination of the two. I can enjoy my own company while still enjoying the comfort of companionship. Silence is

---

([1] W. T. Palmer, *The Verge of Lakeland*, 1938)

an under-used virtue. Appleby always has something to say. How good it is at getting its message across is another matter. It is true that in terms of life outside of its boundaries the town does not shout as loud as it used to do; within its walls it delivers plenty of verbal offerings. Appleby knows what you do, when you do it, and how you did it. If you are busy, it knows. If you are idle, it knows. If you are up to no good, it knows. And if you are worthy of no news, it will give you some. Tea room tabloid banter travels faster than modern-day e-mail, accentuating tales to exercise tongues and tantalise ears. It is said that an innocent hiker who breaks wind crossing the town bridge will, by the "bush telegraph", have succumbed to dysentery by the time they reach the Low Cross.

An extravagant introduction to the social structure of Appleby is important to the understanding of the town and its odd corners. These places are like the people. The people are like the places. Living, breathing, absorbing memories, replaying old tunes. Each has a history, a story to be told. All history books and town guides mould the facts to suit their needs and Appleby

Ice flow on the River Eden. Photograph by John T. Hall.

is no less political in nature. My own interpretation of the town is testimony to my experiences, coloured by a combined genetic instinct and reactionary free thought. These are thoughts borne from naïve childhood influences virgin to territory beyond Appleby's border and of life of a forty-something returning home after two decades of global exploration.

From a conscious junior independence to an eventual late-teen departure, my friends and I knew every corner of Appleby. That's what we thought. We actually only knew what was within our territory and within that secure stronghold. History and tradition were irrelevant.

Appleby was now. We were now. Whether on foot or on popular push bike, we were part of the anatomy of the town. Vibrant corpuscles flooding the veins and charging the natural energy of the town's organs. My choice of odd corners reflects my fond memories of these childhood wanderings and, now, of contemplative recognition over the last year or so. Such observation recognises some change, particularly in social structure and cultural approach. Yet, I must remember that I am viewing it from a different window. My own personality and emotions are different too. On a Gaussian curve of opinion, I still feel strong for just cause, but I now accept "what will be, will be" and am aware of where I can make a difference and where I cannot.

Appleby's people strive to defy the generation gap. Some are born old. Some retain eternal youth. Yet they often fail in this defiance. Respect for elders diminishes through the sad compromise of global mediocrity, while at the other end of the spectrum few of our elders become diplomats for the electronic revolution. In my youth, the town's elders were treated as heroes. And if not, they were anti-heroes. We mocked them of course, like kids do. We did not necessarily aspire to be like them, our ambitions lay dormant. We did admire them however, whether they be Tom Barker, shuffling street-cleaner, Audrey Wappet, larger-than-life Mayoress, Billy "Tutt", sentinel tailor, Reg Folder, iconic antiquities dealer, or Gordon Walton, mortal pantheon of band and railway. These characters, defending their turf and fulfiling rules of Belbinism, are now simple memories to those remaining.

Thankfully, they have been replaced. And some. Witness protagonist Mayor, Lancelot Thwaytes, galvanising socialite, Graham Coles, stoical station master, Bob Parmley, commanding campaigner, Eric Wooff, cheerful caretaker Mike Graham and tireless lioness Ella Langan. Our very own soap characters, bubbling with enthusiasm, are the toast of the town.

I am grateful to have the opportunity to mix philosophy with photographs and add Hayes to the list of the Appleby authors of Hinchcliffe, Holdgate and Holmes. Perhaps, in twenty years time I shall repeat this work to expand on some of today's cameo characters and to revisit, I hope, a few more familiar, and still odd, corners. In the meantime, let us tour today's odd corners, my odd corners, Appleby's odd corners.

BANKSIDE BOOKS

My appreciation of William T. Palmer and other members of the fellowship began here. To me, this vessel of literature is what second-hand book shopping is all about. Bankside Books welcomes the curious explorer seeking an adventure into the unknown. Down a sunless alley above the town's two banks, the door to Phil Higham's shop needs a firm push to enable entry. The shop has no heating, no seating, no coffee and no cake. This is not Ottakars or Waterstones.

Inside, the book room is cramped and unfussy. Bending forward to squint at the literary classics one runs the risk of colliding hinds with rucksack-waving browsers stretching high towards the mountaineering selection on the other side of the narrow room. Hobbies such as gardening and bird-watching are well-sited at eye level, railways and transport can be tracked down by the floor, and items adult in nature inevitably find themselves on a higher platform. Amusingly, Scottish topography is situated above the local Cumbrian books with southern England appropriately on the southern shelves below. Phil knows his stock and, usually, it is well sorted by subject so he is available for interrogation. That said, I still prefer the thrill of the chase, the excitement of the hunt and the pleasure of discovery. To simply ask him: "Have you got so and so by such and such?" defeats the very essence of the pastime. Folk who do that should stick to the high street stores or stay at home and surf the internet.

The challenge to find that elusive tome is made the more demanding by, and all second-hand book shops share this trait, strange and obscure opening times. This is a habit peculiar to many shops in Appleby, and questionable in merit as Appleby is a town dependent on seasonal trade and often hindered in visitor numbers by inclement weather. Coming back to Appleby from a 24/7 time in south-east England left me struggling to cope with the cool-breeze attitude of the town. Kicking dust, however, I emerge in better health, but still occasionally frustrated at the five p.m. and half-day closing, short-houred Saturdays and desert-like Sundays.

Phil's experience at Bankside and understanding of the needs of his customer does mean that he can allow himself to be generous to both the regular clientele and passing trade. Books are fairly priced, especially when compared to book shops in places of high attraction around the country where the infrequent visitor may not return. Good value is to be had at Appleby's other book "store", the Rotary Bookshop. Situated between Spar, the mini-mart and the Royalist public house, the Crown and Cushion, the Rotary shop sells all kinds of stock, donated by townsfolk, in aid of charity. As such, prices are most definitely on the side of the customer and one would be foolish to depart without a bargain or two.

Barry McKay offers antiquarian and limited edition reading at his perfectly named Barry McKay Rare Books, in Battlebarrow. A highly regarded mail order and internet bookseller deserved of mention, he is specialist in nature so I can forgive him for working in a virtual world.

Returning to Bankside, at the back of the shop is a fine selection of assorted bric-a-brac and more books. A menagerie of bits and bobs that may appeal to the collector, that may provide that special elusive gift, or simply make you smile, because whatever it is, it is odd. The larger bric-a-brac items, such as rustic furniture approaching antiquity, rest wind-battered in the alley but successfully avoiding storms, floods and drought. Incidentally, I do enjoy the coffee-offering, sofa-sitting, squeaky-clean high street stores (as long as

I don't have to queue) and occasionally I have even purchased recreational material via the worldwideweb (when technology and plastic permit).

COURTYARD GALLERY

Boroughgate welcomes visitors from the west with trees, planted in 1874, acting as a guard of honour, presenting the main attractions. However, the keen visitor sometimes has to look a little closer for the Town Jewels. Travellers put off by the climb up Boroughgate to the castle easily miss the Courtyard Gallery. A narrow passageway below the White Hart Hotel reveals a lovely setting of chairs and flowers and immediate serenity. It is the ideal location after twisting and turning in Bankside Books or the perfect retreat

from the haphazard Boroughgate traffic.

Appleby has its fair selection of tea rooms and cafes, all of which have their value. The Courtyard Gallery, as the name implies is not a tea room but as hospitality abounds it is a venue where one can sit, relax and imbibe herbal teas (and cake!) while enjoying informal conversation with owner Andrew Wright. Vines and shrubs hang freely over the yard decked with ambient furniture for those wanting solitude after a town tour.

Up the wooden stairs into the gallery, the visitor will find a double room tastefully crammed full of paintings, oils and etchings. No claustrophobia here. Largely stocking work by local artists, and for local read northern, Andrew is well-informed about each work and has an intimate knowledge of many of the artists' skills and styles. The gallery, once a granary, dame school and artist's studio, also stocks a superior collection of ceramics and pottery, glassware and jewellry.

The Courtyard Gallery is a place where I can enjoy my own company in the company of others. The pictures on the wall can lift you out of your yourself into a world of imagination. That dream state company can entice and bewilder. I rather unwisely spent a sum of money, and money I didn't really have, on a nude by Tom Oldham. I don't know why I should blush when Andrew told me the model for the nude had been in for tea, but I did. Strangely, my painting has never been hung and remains turned against a wall in a garage. Three figures of notes on one figure of note was lustfully too extravagant.

HIGH WIEND

The peculiar one-way system around the inner town takes the driver steadily down the narrow street of High Wiend. Protected by a sleeping policeman cautiously funnelling Market Square escapees, driver or pedestrian may wonder what lurks down this hidden corner. The bold letters E.W.S. crop up on many town walls in the region, but none so grand and dictatorial as those directly below the High Wiend street sign. The only "Emergency Water Supply" to be found beyond the arrow is the River Eden as it flows out of Appleby to Bolton and beyond. To picture the river a hundred yards or so from this point is a good reminder of the hairpin loop it must endure from the eastern side of town.

High Wiend has seen much busier times than those it enjoys today. Like its sister road, Low Wiend, the narrow entrance served as a defensive barrier against invasion in troubled times. With townsfolk and livestock bundled into the square, the gap could be easily plugged. In times of local peace the street has seen some activity of commercial value. It is hard to imagine that four public houses (the Black Boy [now Hoagy's Bistro], the Chequers, the Crown and Thistle, and the Golden Ball) entertained an audience devoid of televisual distractions. Only the Golden Ball remains, a gold nugget indeed amongst Appleby's treasures.

The thread of jewellery continues with the astonishing

fact that High Wiend used to house three watchmakers. Times change! In living memory, there has also been a Department of Employment. Befitting the local sense of humour this was often called the Department of Unemployment. County centralisation and diminished work opportunities saw its demise with its executives joining the queue that once fed them.

Today's High Wiend still contributes to contrasting commerce. Functional pet shop, café and launderette feed domestic needs. Serving a transient tourist population the flavour of the commercial premises has had to change and, somewhat sadly, the trades and customs of a century ago are no longer with us. What will the future bring? In another century, will readers be puzzled to hear of pet shop, café and launderette?

In these days of global technology and personal telecommunications, they may find the service of the neighbouring Post Office redundant. Appleby's Post Office belongs to the top of High Wiend in a building built jointly with the Conservative Club in 1912 on the site of a row of cottages, themselves hosting another inn, the Crown and Punchbowl. The current facility may have outlived the large informative notice in the window. I cannot believe that the following facility is still in existence:

> *Telegrams may be dictated from a*
> *kiosk at any time.*
> *The nearest kiosk is*
> *in Borough gate*

Inside the reception is still very much traditional.

The ever-curling queue may place you in an awkward corner, but the warm, friendly approach of the smiling counter staff soon sets in patient mind as the town's latest dramas and incident are discussed. The back room staff may find themselves less cheerful to satisfy the window's other claim:

Letters can be posted after midnight for first delivery at the following places:	
Brampton	*6.30 am*
Knock	*6.30 am*
Dufton	*6.30 am*
Longmarton	*6.30 am*
Great Asby	*6.30 am*
Warcop	*6.30 am*

LOW WIEND

The vast majority of visitors to the town now have to walk along Low Wiend from the relatively new and expanded car park adjacent to King George V's playing field. However, they may be too busy in their early anticipation of seeing the town centre that they forget to pause and observe what lies along Low Wiend itself. The shop units on either side of the road are clearly from a modern age but this does not diminish their appeal.

If Bankside and Courtyard present ephemera, then Doris' Cave reveals a menagerie of miscellany. Her Cave, as the name ventures to imply, is a cluttered cavern of magical second (third, fourth and fifth) hand bric-a-brac emporium that the pleonastic Doris Bainbridge opened a number of years ago to raise money to save the town's swimming pool from closure. She has continued her fund raising and collected more to support the building of a fitness suite aside the pool complex. Doris has quite rightly been awarded an MBE for her efforts.

The "China Moon" Chinese Takeaway is a popular recent addition to the expanding catering options in the town. Chinese, Indian and pizza cuisine is a long way from the "fast-food" alternatives of two fish and chip shops thirty years ago. One of the "chippys", called Eden Fisheries, was run by T. and E. R. Willingale in the building undergoing renovation next to Doris' Cave. A local tale tells of a young lad asking for more chips from the lady behind the counter because he reckoned the fish had eaten his chips the night before. She swiftly put him in his place by sharply replying: "Tell you what lad, I'll save your chips by giving you a smaller fish this time!" The other chippy was Miss Powell's on Bridge Street.

Completing the north side of the street is the building housing, amongst others, the Health Clinic, Day Care Centre and County Library. The library, celebrated its 30th birthday in October 2002, and was the first to move into the building, coming from its previous location up from the A'Board Inn in Boroughgate. At the time of writing, the functions held within the complex are considering whether to remain or move to an expanded site. The need for expansion is clear, particularly with so many health care professionals in service. Appleby's game of musical chairs plays a theme throughout this literal symphony.

On the opposite side of the road is another short parade of retail units including another launderette, the

Emerald Laundry, and an Age-Concern charity shop, again one of two. The wide end of the street used to house Parkin's Warehouse and a short row of terraced cottages. Prior to their demolition I remember stealing into the derelict row as a young boy in a fresh-air gang pushing the limits of dare and counter-dare. Standing on the tarmac hard surface it takes a vivid imagination to reflect that the airspace used to occupy someone's sitting room.

Low Wiend was also the home of Appleby's original Grammar School, granted a Charter by Queen Elizabeth I in 1574, and went by the obvious name of School House Lane. Look for inscriptions in the sandstone

wall running along Chapel Street. These stones origi-
nate from the garden of Reginald Bainbrigg (perhaps
related to Doris?), one of the first headmasters of the
school.

From this end of the street the Eden Community Hall
can be seen as it enjoys a mixture of uses from arm-
raising joyous religious service to arm-raising energetic
power yoga (and tomorrow, it hopes to have an arm-
raising acrophobic climbing wall). Its future, like many
historic buildings, always remains in doubt. Officially
named "Centre '67" when first given over to the town
for youth projects, the hall used to be the Tabernacle
Methodist Church. It is still called Centre '67 by many
and, thankfully, it still holds ideals based on youth

OLD GASWORKS

Or rather no gasworks. At the end of Chapel Street where the River End turns the corner back on itself is the site of the former town gasworks. Originally built in 1837 at a huge cost of around £1500, it stopped as a coal-gas production site in the mid-1960s. Switching to the more efficient butane-air-gas, the automated and regulated gas holder along with a special unit built near Holme Street had a limited life span as the operation became too limiting to accommodate the ever-demanding population.

Only in recent years has the ground been levelled to provide a much needed overflow car park. Sleepy Appleby never one to rush things! The future use of the site is now approved as a Primary Care Health Centre which will revolutionise the quantity and quality of care in our community. The decision is not without controversy as many locals question the demands that will be required from Chapel Street when it comes to weight of traffic.

Appleby is well served by suitable halls (Public Hall, Eden Community Centre) and suitable organisations (Swimming Club, Cricket and Football Clubs, Squash

activities. Its indoor management is overseen by the enthusiastic Eden Community Outdoors team who eloquently parade the needs of the young.

At the narrow end of the street the Crown and Cushion welcomes you back into the town centre. Like High Wiend, the narrow gap was easily plugged in times of invasion. The gap still serves as a barrier. This time the only suffering Scots are those driving Juggernauts that have foolishly chosen a low route (Doomgate against Shaw's Wiend) as their route into town.

Former landlord of the "Cushion" Chris Wilson is someone to search out if the visitor wants to know more about Appleby's pub history. His book *Something Close To My Heart* aptly describes the whereabouts of over fifty hostelries within a three-mile radius from Hoff to Hilton. Sadly, or rather, soberly, most are now dry houses. By strange coincidence, Doris used to live at one of these old inns. The Crown and Falcon, popular with railway navvies at the end of the 1800s, became and still is "Wearisome". It can be found, dethroned and derelict, on its very own corner on the outskirts of Appleby just before Burrells.

Club, Air Training Corps, Girl Guides, Boy Scouts and more). Not a bad collection for a town of under 3,000 residents. Indeed the thriving scout group has a well-equipped hut behind the old gasworks site. For a town suffering with a lack of appropriate car parking options, many people see its current usage as the most appropriate. We shall see.

Also, adjacent is the Appleby War Memorial Swimming Pool. Opening in 1959, the pool was an oasis for kids when I was growing up. Opening at two o'clock and closing at seven in the evening, the core of Appleby's youth would spend five hours getting wet and fit, getting fit and wet. Saturday's gave us an extra two hours, as the pool was open in the mornings from ten until noon. Did this open-air hobby make us hardy

in nature ready for t-shirts and shorts all the year round or are we blessed with fine northern warm blood anyway?

To be a lifeguard was the lofty ambition of frequent users and I am proud to say that this position came my way in my teenage years. Whilst the task also involved cleaning the pool of leaves and hosing-down the concrete sides, it also availed me of the key. I can now confess with recognised good fortune and personal gratitude that I improved my aquatic talents by out-of-hours swimming. I hope I can be forgiven. Finances involved in running a heated seasonal outdoor pool became stretched to breaking point and the all-year-round indoor pool was inevitable. Re-opening in March 1995 the new pool is now enjoyed by young and old whenever they want. Good though it is, somehow it's not the same.

Linking the pool to the gasworks are a series of metal plates lying flat along the edge of the car park. This is part of Appleby's flood defence system called Appleby's Flood Alleviation Scheme. I only point out the name to highlight a possible subtle difference in the words "defence" and "alleviation". It was opened by Steele Addison, chairman of the National Rivers Authority flood defence committee on 27 October 1995.

Three of the seven flood gates, at the pool, town bridge and playing field, are enhanced with themed "water mark" sculptures by artist Lisa Jones. Interesting to those who find them interesting; awkward and irrelevant to those who do not. Their metal component offers a different aesthetic and perhaps this is why they are not perceived as natural as, say, a wood carving or rock sculpture. That same metal is inherent in gas-holder structures and it follows that they too are open to artistic admiration. Whether this would be the case if Appleby's gas-holders were still in place is debatable, but I warrant that there is maybe something

comforting about gas-holders that have genuinely become part of our heritage. The most obvious case being those outside the Oval Cricket Ground in London. A controversial entry may be the set that command the M6 motorway just outside Birmingham that simply serve as a reminder that the driver is, usually stationary, just outside Birmingham. Maybe artistic merit is justified through controversy and, in my mind, this would probably be the case with Lisa Jones' water marks.

Appleby's open air swimming pool, picture by John T. Hall.

MILLENNIUM PLAYGROUND

Appleby is fortunate to have three large playgrounds. The Millennium Playground is one of the more modern additions to the town. It incorporates all of the eternal favourites of swings, roundabout and see-saw, but is decorated with vibrant colours and enjoys complex climbing frames to stir the imagination. Known officially as the Barrowmoor Millennium Park the playground serves to entertain the kids of Barrowmoor and Glebe high in the west of the town above Dowpitt's and Bank's Wood.

Sponsored and supported by local businesses the area was opened by Tinky Winky, Laa-Laa, Dipsy and Po on 22 October 2000. It is with nomadic irony that the Barrowmoor bairns build a tree-house outside the confines of the play area. Their camp patrol tower adds weight to the unfortunate necessity of CCTV cameras.

The quickest, or shortest, way to reach the playground from the town is up the steep path from the Holme Street/Chapel Street/High Wiend intersection.

The struggle up the hill is worth the perseverance as the route also offers a diversion onto foot paths out of town towards Colby Laithes and Bandley or into Dowpitts Wood for a nature trail back down to the river.

Dowpitts Wood offers a wide variety of camouflaged escapism opportunities as an adventure playground for budding soldiers or cowboys or for keen naturalists seeking to twitch or root about. From nippleworts to pignuts, from cleaves to cocksfoot grass, from blackcaps to blue tits and from woodpeckers to willow warblers,

there is much to enjoy. A detailed trail guide is available from the excellent tourist information centre in the Moot Hall.

Back at the playground, the spectacle of the Pennine Fells in the distance is complemented by one of the broadest views of Appleby's landscape. Best seen in winter time when trees are free from foliage, the panorama offers an appreciation of the trek up to the railway station, the landmarks of St. Lawrence's Church and the Grammar School, the comforting high

The old playground, picture by John T. Hall.

arch of Holme Wood contrasting with the flat flood plain of Holme Farm, (once named St. Nicholas' Holme and site of St. Nicholas' Leper Hospital), and the disappearing Eden along the Vale of Tempe.

The Vale of Tempe is shrouded by unknown boundaries and, as a child, it was an area out of bounds. A ghostly land where the risk of not returning was high. The river became larger than life down these bends and would take your life given the chance. The angry current that formed "Whirly", a living legend that promoted lies and tales of "how I swam it", is rarely visited and perhaps wisely so. Respect is given by cartographers who mark the corner as Whirly Lum.

The town's major playground is next to the same river but thankfully by a calmer stretch not far from the bottom of "the Banks" on King George V playing field, more commonly known as the Broad Close, home to the town's football team. The avenue of trees leading to the riverside playground was planted in 1977 to commemorate our Queen's Silver Jubilee This is a fairly new venue for the playground as it used to be sited at the lovely setting of The Butts between the swimming pool and cricket ground. In those days it featured one of the highest banana slides (do children

still call them banana slides?) and tallest swings in the district, with hard floor beneath, the playground became a victim of nervous modernism in the 1990s.

Rumour has it that the playground was moved to its current location for fear of cricket balls rising high for "six" and hitting youngsters at play. If true, we must, belatedly, question this ridiculous decision. Not only has Appleby had few frequent floggers of leather, the same logic would also ban the rural spectator, who as every cricket enthusiast knows, falls asleep within half-an-hour of the game starting. Sandwiched between cricket pitch, swimming pool and flowing river, this was probably one of the safest corners to throw energetic children. Soapbox to one side, I beat a traditionalist's drum and must admit that the "new" playground serves the younger generations well.

Revisiting Barrowmoor and Glebe, the populated expanse of western Appleby, gives us an opportunity to consider the capital invested in bricks and mortar. Today's price for a bungalow on St. Margaret's Way is in the region of £75,000 and climbing. This sets this work in the period of 2002; readers may be reminded below of the cost of a semi-detached bungalow circa 1962 from an advertisement by A. E. Lewthwaite and Son. What price would you give for such a property in forty years time?

Appleby can offer the newcomer a quiet home in a district of natural beauty, with a climate free from extremes... A small building estate is now being developed about ten minutes walk from the centre of the town. Set in pleasant surroundings, it is devoted to labour-saving bungalows designed by an architect to appeal to those of advancing years... Price, at time of going to press is £2300, freehold and including road charges.

SCATTERGATE GREEN AND THE WESLEY TREE

As children growing up in Appleby, Scattergate was a suburb and far out of town. We called the area "Scatty" which was an abbreviation rather than a term of abuse aimed at the residents. Expanding since those days to come close to the Orton road at the top of Parkin Hill in one direction and along the Colby Road in the other, the Scattergate peoples have some of the best views in the town. Overlooking the castle

grounds or the meadows of Rampkin Pastures here exists a micro-community supported by a single shop, One-Stop Scattergate Stores.

A natural vale, Rampkin Pastures has always been prone to flooding and the "suburb" was well worth a visit in the days when winters were longer and harder as the sledging down Halifax Field, on the Colby brow, into the ice rink below was the most thrilling in the town.

Along the avenue of trees that line the main road is a small sycamore that marks the sight of the old "Wesley Tree", blown down in 1961. It was here that

the spiritual father of the Methodist movement, John Wesley stood to preach to countless locals on his tours of the country. The entry from Wesley's own journal reads: *Mon. 30th June 1766 - About two we reached Penrith. Two of our friends guided us thence to Appleby, a county-town worthy of Ireland, containing at least, five-and-twenty-houses.*

Travelling by horse, one cannot deny Wesley's ambition and faith. In the previous week to coming to Appleby, he had visited Glasgow, Dumfries and Whitehaven. In the following two months, he was to preach at Beverley, across Yorkshire, pay a visit to

London, and take in meetings at Bath and Bristol. A mean feat even with today's modern transport options. According to F. B. Chancellor's book of 1955, *Around Eden*, Wesley's first attempt to preach at Appleby had to be abandoned due to wet weather and so he proceeded to Brough and Barnard Castle instead, only to return to Appleby some twenty years later. Interestingly, Wesley refers to Appleby as in the county of Cumberland. With Cumberland and Westmorland as local rivals, in times past and even now, I wonder how such an error was received? I would suggest that

Penrith, thirteen miles away in former Cumberland, now smiles arrogantly at Appleby-in-Westmorland, as Penrith claims administrative control over Eden whilst clearly sitting outside the Eden Valley.

Drivers expecting to gain speed as they exhale themselves out of Appleby through Scattergate must take care as there is a sharp, 90 degree, corner at the foot of Parkin Hill. The odd driver has missed the angle and headed over the edge down Castle Bank towards the river at Bongate Mill. Those successful in taking the bend will rise out of Appleby and pass Parkin Hill Farm

on the right. I was born at the farm in the 1950s and, although I do not remember it, I am reliably informed that as a toddler I was taken to see the uprooted Wesley tree, blissfully unaware that the incident would be retold some forty years later.

JUBILEE

The mill and weir approached from either side of town, Bongate's Mill Hill to the east or Scattergate Green to the west, is one of Appleby's special corners. It is an oasis of particular spiritual energy and cooling tranquillity for locals needing to take "time out". Even passing through with a dog to walk it is difficult not to stop on the bridge and ponder the timeless movement of the water below. The river can corner your senses as perpetual flow mesmerises and brings on odd sensations of swaying and floating.

"Juba" is a natural playground for young children to skim stones, safely paddle, dip nets for bullheads and even swim. In my opinion the best swimming is not as one might expect above the weir, but further downstream opposite the boat house of the castle. Waters gently run over a soft deck of consistent depth. If the thought of an embracing chill is not a wish, then the picnic area offers space to relax and sit in the sun, to listen to the light flow of the water and to peer up with an imagination stirred by the magnificent castle grounds on high.

In 2000, I blessed my new millennium by taking to the waters once more. Near naked with muscles rippling I ventured the waters spending a good hour in aquatic meditation. In truth, the only rippling was from the displaced water and the thrill of being near naked only seemed to entice the attention of a hovering midge cloud. Still, my spirits were lifted.

To the side of the picnic area is one of ten "Eden benchmarks". These are unique sculptures along the Eden Valley from the source at Mallerstang to the Solway Firth at Rockcliffe, they celebrate the splendid river and honour the start of this millennium.

Joss Smith's "Primrose Stone" made from St. Bee's sandstone, is easily one of the best benchmarks along the route. These sculptures have a fair amount of criticism and, indeed, the art critics who consider themselves experts largely dislike the Primrose Stone. It is of no surprise then that it is one of the most popular amongst the lay people who will probably view it from a naïve aesthetic. Naïve, of course, in the eyes of the experts who probably, in some respects only dislike it because of its popularity. Contrast this opinion with the Eden benchmark at Stenkrith near Kirkby Stephen. "Passages" by Laura White courts controversy by critics and general public alike. Does this make it a success?

The field behind the stone is home to the annual Appleby Jazz Festival, founded and organised by Neil Ferber and now in its second decade. Held every summer this now attracts top artists and jazz fanatics from all over the globe. Originally this audible art form took place in the castle arena and enjoyed a totally unique setting. The move to Jubilee has changed the mood but the setting is no less evocative. The 2002 festival featured key performances from experienced stalwarts of jazz like 75-year-old Stan Tracey and upcoming talent such as Ben Castle.

Jubilee is so-named after the bridge built to

acknowledge the 50th anniversary of Queen Victoria's reign. With stepping-stones long gone, the ford barely passable and the original bridge wrecked by the ruthless river the "new" bridge stands firm for all visitors. The plaque beneath the bridge on the Bongate side informs us of its origins:

THIS BRIDGE WAS BUILT IN THE YEAR OF
1970, TO REPLACE THE IRON BRIDGE
ERECTED IN COMMEMORATION OF THE
GOLDEN JUBILEE OF HER LATE
QUEEN VICTORIA IN 1887, AND WHICH WAS
DAMAGED BEYOND REPAIR BY FLOOD
WATERS ON THE 23rd MARCH 1968.
OFFICIALLY OPENED BY THE WORSHIPFUL
THE MAYOR OF APPLEBY
ALDERMAN D. MACDONALD
ON THE 1st APRIL 1971

CEMETERY AND POTCHEFSTROOM MEMORIAL

Opposite the Royal Oak Hotel and above Mill Hill sits the oft-unnoticed Potchefstroom Memorial. Strange that it remains unnoticed and invisible as it stands on the corner of the main road into town and is passed by many pedestrians on their way to or from the river at Jubilee. Listing the soldiers who perished as "Appleby Active Service Volunteers" in the Boer War South African conflict of 1900-1901, the memorial proudly puts Thomas Leonard Atkinson in pride of place:

ERECTED
BY PUBLIC SUBSCRIPTION
IN MEMORY OF
THOMAS LEONARD ATKINSON
B COMPANY 2nd V.B.
BORDER REGIMENT, WHO DIED AT
POTCHESFSTROOM SOUTH AFRICA
JUNE 18th 1900.
WHILE SERVING WITH THE
VOLUNTARY ACTIVE SERVICE
COMPANY OF THE BORDER
REGIMENT.
FOR QUEEN AND COUNTRY.

The soldiers remembered on the other side of the monument reflect surnames of families still common to this part of the world: Atkinson, Davey, Gibson, Holme, R. Howe, T. Howe, Robinson, Saul, Slack, Tydd, and Woof.

The horse trough built into the sandstone wall behind the monument echoes a similar age of hard work and devotion to duty. Betrayed by the erosion of time, it too stands as a monument to life without our modern conveniences. The wall, containing artifacts and folly work from previous restoration efforts, provides the ideal perimeter to Appleby's mother church, St. Michael's, declared redundant in 1975.

The early 1970s were a grim time for a shrinking town. In 1974 local government reorganisation saw Appleby's loss of the status of Borough, which it had held for nearly 800 years, and the old counties of Westmorland and Cumberland were joined in unwilling matrimony as Cumbria. In protest local residents changed their address to "Appleby-in-Westmorland."

St. Michael's now has secular use as home to a local artist and his family. During May and June of 2002 its doors were opened once more as part of the Eden Open Studios initiative. This initiative saw a further 40 professional artists at 27 Eden sites of homes, halls, barns, and studios presenting their works to the viewing public.

Having seen much of the exhibition I may be cornered to admit some of it as falling into the "odd" category. Of course, as this book testifies, defiance of convention can lead to perceptions of weird and wonderful, even odd, particularly in the field of art and literature. Testimonials confirm that if attractive to the individual, whether through social conditioning or radical free thought, it, the art in question, fulfils its duty.

Behind the cambered corner of the rising main road, lies Back Lane. This foot route is one of the three available to access the grounds of Appleby's Cemetery. Cross Croft offers the only vehicular route, while pedestrians can also take to Drawbriggs Lane and reach

the cemetery by, carefully, crossing the Settle to Carlisle railway track.

It is natural to think of such places as sad and solemn places, and rightly so. However, they can be places of great interest where the weary traveller can find somewhere to sit quietly to ponder life's vicissitudes. The curious traveller can respectfully wander between grave stones, seeking and imagining the lives of those lost to us. With railway and former Express Dairy buildings in the foreground, those at peace have magnificent views of the Pennine Fells, in particular the masterful Cross Fell.

The town's memorial to its soldiers of the First and

Second World War is a limestone pillar set in the centre of the cemetery. The memorial march of Appleby Town Band at the British Legion Parade used to climb to the monument in the cemetery. However, from 1972, they had to limit their gentle-gaited procession to an inner town route when band members who were veterans of the First World War found the Bongate itinerary too much for their given limbs. Unfailing in activity the Town Band remains on top form and still bangs the drum for all town events, celebratory and memorial.

The observant traveller will notice that the cemetery is not too many departures away from completing its allowance of permanent visitors. Originally laid down in 1910, the authorities have it in their upcoming diaries to review capacity and consider expansion or alternative sites.

It will be difficult to find such a respectful corner. If Jubilee offers a spiritual reminder of the things that are beautiful on this Earth, then the cemetery deals a card from the same pack but with the recognition that our time on this land is not permanent. The value of every day, a gratitude and an understanding, beckons with ever-increasing clarity as I not only witness icons of my childhood laid to rest, but gently observe stone reminders of those forever younger than myself now headed on an unknown journey.

KINGDOM HALL

Hewn into the sandstone rock face against the road in Bongate as it drops onto The Sands is the home of Appleby's Jehovah's Witnesses. Like many other buildings in the town its site and structure are considered completely normal because of their longevity in the memory. It must have been quite an ambitious achievement to consider and succeed in building the preaching house in such a location, as it is carved out of a solid sandstone cliff. Previously known as Rock Chapel, built in 1872, the intention to place it in a position perfect for propaganda, capturing the passer-by on their way in or on their way out of town showed typical religious fervour and belief.

Today, it is doubtful that potential new recruits to prayer are able to stop for service as their speed hovers suspiciously above the legal thirty miles an hour limit passing the high Hall. The official entrance is now protected, in part, from racing traffic by being on the road above and behind the building.

The previous uses of the Hall seem to confirm its likely suitability for the practices of faiths considered by many to be left (or right) of centre. The Primitive Methodists used the facility until 1936 before merging, through the 1932 Deed of Union, with the Wesleyan Methodists and collaborating with the congregation at the Sand's Methodist Church (built 1888).

Without formal religious basis, but with no doubt, a procedure of ceremony and protocol, the Pembroke Lodge of the Manchester Unity of Oddfellows also took a turn in this odd corner before a short term of private use and then, in 1979, the current incumbents. The Jehovah's Witnesses refurbished the building giving it a new second floor for the meeting room, and a new entrance from the top side, enabling the closure of the exposed front steps. Perhaps unfairly, the faith and

practices of the Jehovah's Witness peoples is sometimes treated with wary unease. A feeling of matters unknown through ignorance or unfortunate experience is bound to instill discomfort. I hesitate to use the term odd to define the sect, as my own experience is very limited. Indeed, like many of Appleby's residents, I have never seen inside Kingdom Hall nor attended a service. I expect elements of xenophobia solicit hesitation in revealing Socratic irony.

Within the rural communities of Great Britain there is still much praise given to God, albeit courting metronomic degrees of revival or ruin. Appleby is clearly no exception as, even with the demise of the aforementioned St. Michael's Church and the Tabernacle Methodist Chapel, the town is well endowed with religious establishments including St. Lawrence's Church, the Sand's Methodist Church, the Roman Catholic Church of Our Lady of Appleby, Eden Community Church, the Kingdom Hall and even the devotional group the Baha'i Faith of Appleby. There are many places to offer salvation, hope and wisdom for Appleby's sinners!

Most people do not enter into spiritual gymnastics once they have found their route following their questioning period, usually in youth or early maturity. Their lot does not see them publicly defending nor opposing their faith. Individual spirituality remains a private affair. The company of ritualistics combine, predominantly on Sundays, to provide enlightenment for routine daily duties and inner strength in times of crisis. Our modern habit is often to look at religion from the point of belief rather than that of practice.

Still, with so many faiths, it would be easy to assume that Appleby people are a virtuous caring society. Yet, comforts of ridicule and inverted gamesmanship are commonplace, especially in today's society of blame. Trends or fashions, influenced by the media and global tensions, may be responsible, as are undoubted feelings of insecurity.

It would be satisfying to identify Appleby's townsfolk to be above such characterisation. They are not and the town has its own favourites and flavours of the month that defy their place on the spectrum of good and bad. I feel it is important to state this unless I was to give the impression of its peoples to be entirely unique, flawless and deserving of any heavenly rewards heading their way. To warrant acceptance of such controversial thinking, I have to admit to co-operative patronage taking my own sermon as an extension between affection and contempt.

Set in the sandstone rock, as the road beneath Kingdom Hall curves towards town is a ramshackle bolted gate that used to belong to the Howgatefoot blacksmith. Horses for "shoeing" would queue on the road as he applied his trade. Today the contents behind the gate are hidden from the wanderer, but the front does offer itself as an aesthetic artefact for the keen photographer. However, such keenness must be matched with care as this busy corner offers little relief from thundering transport tickling the toes of pausing pedestrians.

CORONATION PARK

On The Sands past the Police Station (the sign efficiently says Constabulary Station) and beyond the neighbouring Mews Cottages, but before the old St. Michael's Church Institute (currently under redevelopment as residential dwellings) is the passage through to Coronation Park. A short rise up steep steps and a small copse of trees greets the visitor who could only really find the park by accident.

Amongst the mature trees along well-laid paths is a small playground, upgraded in recent times to include the now expected climbing frame and apparatus similar to that found on the Broad Close and Barrowmoor playgrounds. Today's agile youngsters do miss one thing though; in my childhood days the area used to have a sand pit.

The land was originally donated to the town by Alderman James F. Whitehead, to be laid out as parkland for the people of Appleby in response to the request for a playground for the children of this side of town. Alderman J. N. Ewbank then prevented ageism by contributing the seats for the benefit of the older population. The park may be taken for granted as a route to town by residents of Castle View Fields (an estate built on the former Auction Market when agriculture and

railway trade were married to great effect), but I suspect that its measured nature gives pleasant air to all users, aware or not.

Below the park is one of the highest and imposing walls in Appleby (castle excepted) that clearly served as a suitable deterrent to prisoners of the police cells behind and to inhabitants of the former Appleby Gaol. The Police Station, notably referred to as the Cop Shop has a past worthy of mention. In 1972, the same period as Appleby lost much of its county status and responsibilities, the police station interior and cells were demolished and rebuilt as seen today.

Only the frontal facade remains of the gaol buildings erected on the site in 1771. The renowned architect Robert Adam had prepared plans, in 1767, for a complex of town hall, county court and gaol but it seems that Appleby was as frugal with its budget in those days as it is today. The grandest municipal buildings were slowly diminished as plan after plan was submitted. Adams' plans were replaced by the more modest structures of Robert Fothergill, a local man.

Eventually, the complex did include the Shire Hall, home to the tiny but important Assize Court (until 1970), and was built for a princely sum of £357.00.

This is another historic building with an uncertain future, but an enthusiastic group of loyal townsfolk, born and bred Applebians and welcomed in-comers, have formed a group called Appleby Legacy with the key aim to give the moribund Shire Hall a new purpose. Campaigners are trailing the way for a romanticised Gypsy Museum. Other suggestions have included a home for Railway memorabilia based on Appleby's Settle to Carlisle connections, an Appleby Arts Centre, a national centre for the Knitting and Crochet Guild or even, perhaps, a timely and efficient complete demolition to spare room for much needed car parking facilities.

Whilst I occasionally like to rattle cages and play Advocate to the Devil, I have no strong views on the outcome, as long as the town is able to capture praise for being pro-active and can shrug off any notion of somnolence. The mayor and town council, the Appleby-in-Westmorland Society and the many clubs and groups that rally to causes are the mortar between the bricks of the town. Giving their all to maintain viability and purchase they still need the support of common stonework to survive. In other words, and in roving Romany parlance, I hope their efforts are not akin to flogging a dead horse.

The muezzin mayor may yet prove talisman to the town's epochal viability. The site is enjoying much publicity, both locally and nationally. Channel 4's television programme *Time Team* visited the premises in October 2002 to excavate the yard area behind the police station.

The site of the old gaol was discovered along with a treadmill used for both exercise and punishment. Also unearthed were the quarters used by the female prisoners. Rather than exploiting the opportunity for gratuitous television and simply the digging for bones, the anthropological experts were investigating the effects of legislation on reform for management of criminals. Such publicity will hopefully garner new visitors to the town whether it is to witness progress with the Legacy project, to tackle all of Appleby's tourist options, or to take part in the next gypsy gathering.

The 2002 New Fair boosted the town's sheckles as visitors and travellers rode in with lively anticipation having missed out a year earlier due to the foot and mouth crisis. Whilst numbers were high, days were short and the crowds disappeared promptly as the rains came down. There is now talk of making the event a weekend festival. What damage this might do to trade and any notion of a successful Romany Museum is unknown. One thing is clear, the town will need plenty of lucky horse-shoes for the legacy to thrive.

BELLEVUE IN LADY GARTH FIELD

It may stretch journalistic licence to mention Athens and its perimeter of hills alongside the natural geography of the Appleby landscape. However such an anthropological comparison is not entirely without merit, albeit on a much smaller scale. Whilst hardly purveying seven hills of political power and mythical lore, there is no doubt that the centre of Appleby is surrounded by higher ground. It is impossible to get out of the town without going up. Whether it be Battlebarrow or Bongate, or the Banks or Boroughgate, or out to Burrells or Barrowmoor, the journey must take the wanderer to a higher turf.

The reader may still struggle to compare to Athenian might. I contest that the comparison is more than just one of physical ground and rests in a metaphysical relationship, to which the Greek Empire made flavour. The people from Appleby's strange hills take on the characteristics of their closest neighbours, themselves victims of environmental transference over the ages. As such, we get a Battlebarrow breed who differ from the bastions

of Bongate, who themselves are a mile away from their brothers across the river on the other side of town.

Perhaps I have slipped from journalistic licence into poetic licence, yet I know that, as kids, there was immense territorialism and tremendous rivalry between "suburbs." Now of older years, I can appreciate the charm and character of these hills and in particular, I feel a soft spot for Bellevue. Sandwiched between Clifford Street and Pembroke Street above "Lady Garth's", Bellevue offers one of Appleby's steepest hills and a rare escape route out of town.

If my Greek analogy was made of myth then it may not be so overtly ambitious to draw parallels with the prosperity of York due to the arrival of the railway and the growth of Appleby during the same period for the same reason. Prior to the arrival of the railways, this side of Appleby must have been under-utilised and foreboding because of its slopes. Both the Eden Valley Line and the Settle to Carlisle line forced that area of the town to develop. The trident raking of Clifford Street, Bellevue and Pembroke Street lined the climb below the stations and a new suburb was born. It must have been quite a sight from the Appleby side of the river. As if dropped from the air, the social dynamics of the town had a new partner to contend with.

The new houses were an island on the bank and needed to be given a bridge into the town. It is well reported that in 1886 the town's corporation put forward a plan to purchase the field below, known as Lady Garth Field, and provide the new residents with decent access to the bridge and town itself. Such a path would, of course, help town bound visitors arriving by train to make there way down. The Local Government Board did not approve a loan for the purchase (it wasn't easy then either!) and consequently several burgesses bought it privately from Lord Lonsdale's trustees. Lady Garth's was born and the whole area prospered thanks ultimately to the railways. A further example of expansion due to the railways was the opening of the Auction Mart near Appleby West on 29 May 1876.

Bellevue is unique amongst Appleby's streets. Its sisters of Clifford and Pembroke may be tight neighbours but their only real similarity is their shared gradient. The latest homes in and around Appleby bear even less common ground. Bland is not a fair word to use to describe the estates of Castle View Fields, Glebe and Barrowmoor. Indeed they hold a certain spell in their spiral designs. Yet their character is a mere shadow of that seen in Bellevue. Some would say that the street belongs to a different town, but it does not, it belongs to Appleby. With the "beautiful view" in mind I may, in this modern age, only be romanticising from a position behind the camera; one thing is true however, isolation above Lady Garth Field is left in the distant past.

HERITAGE CENTRE

At first glance, the good's shed down the track from Appleby West looks like a resting-place for old wagons and carriages of a bygone age. That glance does not betray the vision for it is an old good's shed and it is a resting-place for old wagons and carriages. Yet it is more. Vision is what a wise owl with business acumen and a desire to help others tread the same boards has displayed. The old site, long since dismantled of its railway function, is now the Appleby Training & Heritage Centre.

This dedicated learning centre serves the whole community. It is for anyone who has the desire or need to enhance their personal knowledge and skill profile, or simply satisfy demands of a new hobby. Putting a workshop into a good's shed makes complete common sense. What better place to restore an old carriage than in its original home?

Originally opening in 1995 the Centre came into its own with the acquisition and refitting of a number of carriages. Since then the focus of the education programmes run from within the carriages are computer

related classes along with practical skills such as engineering and woodwork. Whether learning to gain a recognised qualification (to enhance employment opportunities) or simply learning for fun (to keep up with the grandchildren) the computer classes are attended by young and old.

I speak from personal experience when I say that the environment is ideally suited to learning. The novel location is very different to the typical classroom offered by academic institutions. Learning has long been identified almost exclusively with what happens in the school environment. The only difference is sometimes applied to adult education and even that is dimly shifted to academic institution or worse, hotel conference rooms. The challenge of change has been accepted by few and it takes courage to create new learning environments in place of the typical linear approaches.

The railway carriage is not a new concept. It has been tried and tested with success across the world at schools in Australia and closer to home at the National Railway Museum in York where the National Curriculum is combined with interactive learning techniques. Perhaps one of the most exciting lessons is on

board a moving train near Utrecht where a Dutch railway company has added an extra carriage for students. Like all opportunities, the train will always leave the station, it is up to the individual when to climb on and when to step off.

I am currently studying for a City and Guilds Diploma in Information Technology, with special focus on database management, and I haven't yet had to stay behind or do extra homework. It must be the apple I bring in every day for teacher! My classroom comrades each study different disciplines. Like me, their eyes shift in rigid focus from screen to work book and back again, joining the revolution unsure if the spoils of the battle will exceed their effort. So, ponderously charged, my learning companions brave the virtual new world with hesitant enthusiasm. One noble act is copied by many, as we all, in turn, confess to the struggle by raising a hand and asking for assistance. Honesty is rewarded as the draining task of "going back to school" commands due praise and support from loyal tutorage. Fears are soon dispelled as everyone settles to realise their own learning pace (usually above expectations).

Courses can be customised to suit the needs of the individual, under the expected conditions of "term time", course material and class size. Whilst some courses can involve off line work at the student's own home (and at their own pace), I prefer the carriage environment. Every computer has a window view, either the sunny side or track-side. Of course, the tutor cannot guarantee sunshine nor ensure that the living trains run on time!

Appleby has roots in education and is not dormant in making the best use of the population's thirst for knowledge and skills. The Grammar School and Heritage Centre are complemented to great effect by the many special interest groups such as the Embroiders Guild and the long-standing Eden Valley Field Club. The Heritage Centre is not open to the general public, but I do know that if time permits, their helpful staff are happy to allow visitors to view the workshop where the restoration and craft projects are undertaken. Failing that, a good view of the carriages is obtained from the path running by the side of the Centre. This route also gives an alternative variation to the trip back into town.

APPLEBY EAST LEVEL CROSSING

With such a name, we can easily identify a railway theme. But why Appleby East? Many visitors to the glorious Settle to Carlisle line are unaware that Appleby's railway station is in fact Appleby's second station. Appleby East, on the Eden Valley Line, preceded it by some fourteen years before its closure to passengers in January 1962. Indeed the current Appleby Station used to go by the name of Appleby West before its solo duties made the distinction irrelevant.

Appleby East served as a vital link between the North East and the West Coast lines. From Clifton near Penrith the line joined the South Durham and Lancashire Union Railway at Kirkby Stephen and the two enjoyed, and still do, the merged name of the Stainmore Railway. Access to the station itself is now forbidden as the ground is used for a thriving scrap yard.

However, the level crossing stands intact. Silent and still for four lonely decades it lies dormant as if waiting

for its peak-capped signalman to stir the gates back into life. The signal box, bearing the same name, has gone, but the gates remain untouchable as a memorial to the age of steam.

There is much stirring afoot further down the line as the Eden Valley Railway Trust endeavours to bring the line into the 21st century. Cumbria and neighbouring counties are enjoying successful times in regenerating interest and value in our old lines. In addition to the Trust, we can also see much activity by the Stainmore Railway Company (at Kirkby Stephen East), in Wensleydale (from Hawes Junction on the Settle-Carlisle) and lively machinations involving the Penrith

to Keswick link.

Enthusiasts or anoraks, or both, one cannot deny the will and stamina behind the growing number of people wanting to re-ignite this part of our heritage. The railways brought prosperity to towns like Appleby and, in terms of tourism they still do today. Many books and memorabilia exist extolling the virtues of our railway heritage, so that information will not be leaving from this platform.

Architecture has a cultural value. This is beyond dispute. The debate opens when aspects of art and nature are brought together alongside functionality. Many people enjoy the Eden benchmarks, some find them unsightly and some, with accepting aesthetics, consider them a waste of "public money". We can assume that such attitudes were in evidence when stone circles such as Long Meg and her Daughters were erected, or when castle keeps were built high and cairns placed atop mountains. Or perhaps the attitudes were the same when war memorials and swimming pools and millennium monuments celebrated achievements of the time.

Railway architecture fits squarely into this context. Man's invention and initiative is rewarded in structures like Dandry Moss Viaduct at Garsdale and the determined line of the Long Drag in Mallerstang. They are

permanent parts of our cultural heritage. Tied up in tradition and a governing core of ancestral survival, we fight for their preservation. Anticipated prosperity greeted our relics with welcoming arms as industrial revolution promised wealth. Some social commentators of the day, such as Lakeland expressionist John Ruskin, were less than complimentary:

There never was more flagrant nor impertinent folly than the smallest portion of ornament in anything concerned with railroads or near them. Keep them out of the way, take them through the ugliest country you can find, confess them for the miserable things they are, and spend nothing upon them but for safety and speed.[1]

Yesterday's landscape pleases with memories of the past, but it can also heed many a warning. Victoriana can skew the sepia tinted recall. To me, seaside resorts blow sandless shudders. Has anyone been to Morecambe recently? This delayed demise should be a lesson in aforethought to Appleby. Thankfully Appleby's roots dig deeper and whilst similarly built on sand, Appleby's is firm not quick. Today's tourist revolution must be fed by designs with aesthetics in mind. These need not be new, like the Eden benchmarks, although these do form the foundation of tomorrow's attraction. Railways provide escapism to history and as such satisfy a natural yearning for my wide screen eye. Open or closed, the gates are a railway ornament. Their place being symbolic of our past, present and even our future.

[1] John Ruskin, *The Seven Lamps of Architecture*, 1849

TOP ROAD

The argumentative reader will care to move briskly on as they may not consider the Top Road to feature a corner and would question its value in oddity. Move on, that is your choice. The same choice befits the locals and tourists who choose not to venture high out of Appleby, above the Railway Station and by-pass, but prefer to stay below the comfort line at, or just above, river level.

Bedecked in history as Appleby is, it still takes some imagination to picture the Roman engineer building this straight and narrow route from Stainmore to the Scottish Border. Complement that image with the Roman soldier marching through inclement weather to an unwanted posting in far-flung northern climes. The detachment is made easier when taking in the immortal (i.e. in man's lifetime) skyline of Lakeland to the west, Pennines to the east and Dales to the south. Without focus, such distractions may disappear and be forgotten under the constant droning hum of Appleby's by-pass below. Opened in 1981 to save the town from increased structural deterioration and the townsfolk from physical

damage, the by-pass sadly contributes to tiresome noise pollution. You are either someone who can block it out or someone who cannot.

Hopefully I have already persuaded a number of readers to keep away from Appleby's own Fair Mile[1] and leave it undisturbed for the handful remaining to enjoy. Dog-walkers, Sunday morning strollers, foot soldiers of many interests can approach the Top Road, also known as Roman Road or High Street, from many directions. The full route from the town centre, up the Banks, down Colby Road past Scattergate, across Jubilee, up Bongate and Cross Croft, along the Top Road, down Long Marton Road, Battlebarrow and the Sands is roughly three and half miles. The perfect distance to keep an active mind and body, and healthy dog.

I can say from experience that the walk is never the same. Even if the route does not vary the weather will. When, unlikely as it is, the weather maintains consistence the time of day can change from Pennine dawn to Lakeland sunset. And yes, you can meet people with the same idea, and ideals. When, finally, boredom sets in, there is always the option of going the other way around.

The top road is home to the Appleby Manor Hotel. A bland attempt at a grand title and not in truth befitting

the nomenclature of the town. I much preferred its previous name - The Garbridge. Our language is corrupted by corporate manipulation, which I accept to be part of our literal evolution, but it does not mean that I have to like it. I feel it serves to dilute the individuality of identity. A safety-net for our insecure society bombarded by Orwellian fashion and the easy option.

Those wishing to stretch themselves a little more may like to discover the redundant retort from the old gasworks. A five-foot tall iron structure rescued and recycled to find a home as a gatepost just off the Top Road down Hungrigg's Lane a few yards past Stank Lane. The reincarnated retort has now passed into redundancy once more as the gatepost is no longer functional. Whither it's next life? It is discoveries like this that make the road so much of an adventure.

The road only offers this luxury for 51 weeks of the year. For one week in early June the tourists invade in search of the annual Gypsy Horse Fair (or Appleby's New Fair). Like the castle, its tale is told elsewhere, although it is worthy for the record books to mention that the Fair was absent in 2001 due to the foot and mouth tragedy. Only the plague had prevented the gypsy occupancy in the past. The resilient travellers had been permitted to take their place during the last foot and mouth epidemic in 1967 (and in 1922 before

[1] The other narrow Roman Road is the Fair Mile along the Lune Valley in the Howgills.

that), but modern times dictate as administrators from afar cast their power. The busiest Fair in living memory (allegedly) hit our door steps in 2002, yet I have absolutely no doubt that reason will be found to cancel the New Fair once more in my lifetime, and for reasons too odd to invent today; if it captures your curiosity take a tour while you can!

The Roman Road vaguely assists the historians in their estimation of Appleby's past. As a "Top Road" the Romans avoided the town, presumably they found little use for its location. Had they wanted a commercial centre they would have built dwellings at the site of the road. Had they needed a defence then the road would

have dipped towards looping river. Not until the Norman town planner cast his eye over the town as a suitable military setting did Appleby blossom. Later, in more peaceful times, the market town evolved.

Today, the by-pass is the Roman Road in all but name. Distracting champions of haste, the off-road commerce suffers once more. Perhaps Appleby's Romanic popularity was limited by the presence of a major junction at Kirkby Thore (Braboniacum). The Roman Causeway entering the county of Westmorland over Stainmore passed directly to Brougham Castle near Penrith. At Kirkby Thore the Maiden Way took off to Cross Fell and into Northumberland. But a junction

alone does not make a town and Kirkby Thore has since settled for a slumber of it's own.

Controversy remains as history is unclear how the Roman's named Appleby. Campden supposed "Aballaba" whereas Horsley defended "Galacum" with some worth. An unlikely connection is made by Blackmore whose prose from Camelot and King Arthur refer to Aballaba and Appleby in the same breath. Coming from recent research at Rochester University it offers weight with alphabetical authority.

Incredibly my limited research even linked Aballaba and Appleby to Friedrich II of Prussia in the 18th century. When does historical hearsay become fancied fact? The definition, if not the site, is clear. Balla being a town and Ba a bank, Aballaba was "the town on the bank." Many modern thoughts prefer Campden as Bainbrigg's tablets in the wall at Low Wiend refer to Aballaba. Perhaps a keen detective will take time to investigate the under walked equine way from Hangingshaw to Powis and provide us with a relic reminder and challenge to the history books. Myth, legend or truth, for the time being, I too prefer Sweet Home Aballaba. I should, of course, remind the reader that the most common definition of Appleby comes from the old English/Norse "aeppel/eph" for apple and

"by" a simple village or hamlet.

Whether the Romans marched straight past Appleby or paused to meditate is unclear. We do know that the Romany families have taken camp and continue to do so. If there is something to be held in the Antonine Itinerary and the wisdom of Marcus Aurelius then it must lie in the conduit symmetry of heritage. Our legacy and heritage is nothing without the people to foster fragrant past.

Immediately the mind is led on to brotherhood as a possession of self and part of the process whereby self becomes "as a god though no one would be aware of it." Already we are discovering that the synthesis between self's striving for serenity and a policy of humility begins in our life with others. In different words, we are called to serve our brothers with zeal in order that self may make its very own the things belonging to self. Social consciousness becomes devotion to society in the sense that with all its defects and usurpations it is the prime agency for enabling the single life to fulfil the demands made on it by the larger consciousness. The hegemony of the spirit is found to depend on service to society as long as incarnation endures. Worldly humility could not be emphasised more convincingly.[1]

---

[1] Archibald Weir, *For To-day - Modern Thoughts Secured on the Fame of Marcus Aurelius*, 1933.

[1] *History of Appleby*

BRIDGE 239

As the top of Battlebarrow heads up and out towards Penrith there is a swift corner, past the Grammar School, into Long Marton Road, Romany Way and Belgravia. Streets boxed between the railway and by-pass. The corner is dominated by the incredible engineering feat of railway bridge number 239. I am sure it is the whale-like mouth of the bridge that attracts drivers into the gaping tunnel.

Regurgitating them round the exit corner, drivers speed believing they have left the town and head on to Clickham and Brampton. Only when calmed do they realise that the turning to Penrith has eluded them and a return trip under the bridge is inevitable. Indeed, on two occasions in recent months have I been tramping past Croft Ends to be assailed by confused motorists with the question: "Is this the way to Rheged?"

With a base of heavy sandstone blocks and a topping of spiralling red bricks, the astounding construction takes the breath away. It is, quite simply, the work of

the embankment like preposterous propellers ready to beat and fly. Light shading to the pink sandstone tip towards the Grammar School entrance reveals the scars of a structural weakness when, decades ago, flesh of the beast rushed into the road. When standing in the intoxicating maw, for it is "in" rather than "under", it even exudes its own peculiar atmosphere. The air changes. The smell changes. Like a giant beast sloth-like in movement and gesture, it actually appears to breathe. Odd, that on cold, damp days it even sweats. To some, of course, it is just a bridge.

If like me, the structure fills you with wonder, then it will not be long before other bridges are sought. From simple ancient Clapper bridges (nearby Waterhouses is a good example) to modern Millennium monuments (try Skenkrith over the Eden near Kirkby Stephen). From redundant railway relics (Smardale Viaduct in Smardale Gill stuns) to more on the Settle to Carlisle line (compare 239 with its sister, 236, on Drawbrigg's Lane). Walk up the road to stand inside road bridge 806 - a modern construction of no heart. Yet, stand for long enough and there may be just a whisper of life behind the bland concrete slabs that stand efficiently and functionally in place.

The engineers of 239 would have gasped in awe at such a construction. In five more decades visitors may acknowledge 806 as an artistic creation. What can we expect from future bridge builders? The only thing we can be sure of is that it will be different from 239 and 806.

art to prove my earlier conjecture. Before the by-pass was with us, the road curling snake-like beneath was host to the entire A66 traffic and would endure, without effort, a constant stream of heavy vehicle thundering by. On top of this, excuse the pun, the daily roll call of train and loaded wagon above can only confirm its strength.

Built by the Midland Railway over a 125 years ago, one cannot deny its majesty; a railway monument that rivals Batty Moss Viaduct and Blea Moor Tunnel for personal immediacy. Winged abutments taper and hug

HAIR DRESSERS

There must be countless hairdressing salons in Appleby, yet there is only one barbershop. It would be foolish of me to ask why, but I will. Why? Is the population so elderly that the female numbers dominate so? Has today's world of unisex reached this sleepy Pennine town? Does the weekly orbit of the town's women folk have to include stealth like sidestep into the salon? I am sure there are many reasons for such a bias and I am not going to risk my reputation on supposing the reason. It makes the world go around and we should be happy with that notion.

The Ladies Hairdresser at the bottom of Station Road contrives to make this an odd corner of the town. Imagine the virtuosity of a modern mind believing such a site would make a suitable home for hairdressing. Supposedly built with the hands and direction of an itinerant Italian prisoner-of-war who lived out Crackenthorpe way, this Hairdressing Salon sees people trek over from the western Ward across the river to enjoy the social interaction and capture news from the eastern Ward. In the same manner, customers of stylists on the west will come from the east. The local

news network has to work in many ways.

In front of the building is a fine seat. Odd in its own right as it gives walkers a prophylactic breather before they head off up Station Road or Battlebarrow. This used to be the site of the public water supply at the spring of Spout Lane. Before 1877 Appleby's water supply came from several pumps and wells and was "bad in quality and insufficient in quantity."[1]

Having provided a new water supply to the town at a cost of £5,500 the authorities decided to tackle the sanitary arrangements which were described as "deplorable." For some reason there was a great deal of opposition to this scheme but it was successfully completed in 1882.

The view from this seat is pleasant enough, though the traffic demographics have long since altered thus preventing hobby-ist observations. As lads we would sit and collect the names and numbers of heavy haulage vehicles. Do you remember the Border trucks, where each lorry was prefixed with Border and given its own unique name? It was a mile ahead of the current trend of Stobart and Dentressangle.

I also fondly remember that this was the corner where Arnison's Pop wagon would stop. Those days are long gone. Sadly the only common traffic seen on the corner are the little wheels belonging to little brains of the town's young bucks as they flirt with the bored,

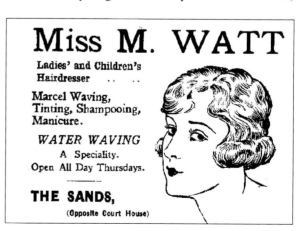

Edmonson's grocers and bakery. This was frequented by your author as a child wanting to spend his pocket money on a hot sausage roll. They also used to make the most delicious brown bread I've tasted - sadly the recipe is long lost.

Below this is Slapestone House, grand for a "terraced" house and full of a vast history relating to St. Mary's Priory up the hill. The lesser door to the right of Slapestone (number 4a) used to be part of the grand house. Indeed the upper rooms still extend over the property. Ancient architects must turn in their grave to see such works diminished for the sake of population demographics. Slapestone was my home after leaving Parkin Hill, from 1963 to adulthood, and only now do I respectfully acknowledge my childhood privilege of eat, sleep and play in such an interesting abode.

Back to the barber and short back and sides. Reuben's crew has been cut under the Moot Hall since 1990. Reputedly the oldest barbershop premises in Westmorland, Reuben was preceded by the town's barber of some thirty-four years, J. Scott, picking up his scissors in 1956 he took the advertising tag line of "Gentlemen…. My Business Grows on You!"

and boring, young does. Slaves to Mercury, God of Speed, these motors parade at a maddening tempo performing ritualistic circuits hoping to impress. They don't. Life is too short, better courtship fancies would be granted if they were to sit awhile.

The seat on this corner offers views of this historical micro-suburb. The house behind is dated 1662. Across the road is the large window once belonging to

A casual glance through the old Appleby guide books of the 1960s and 70s throws up some equally snappy (or should I say snippy) slogans:

Ladies ! ! !
CONSULT
MAUREEN SNAITH
Hair Stylist
FOR
PERMANENT WAVES, EUGENE, JAMAL, SUPERMA, BRUSHWAVE
HAIR TINTING AND RAZOR CUTTING
Address:
THE SANDS
(Above Spooners' Garage)   Telephone 225

or how about:

WE HAVE A FLAIR FOR IT !

The Hairstyle to

Heighten

Your Personality

Make Your Appointment with

**KATE
WINTER**

TELEPHONE 447

THE DEAD SHOP

If you follow the river along the Sands towards Holme Wood and as the river starts to corner into the tight loop there sits one of Appleby's strangest, oddest, buildings. Again, to those walking past every day it simply exists as part of the furniture of Battlebarrow. The square red-brick, two-storey building served most of its life as the town's mortuary. As boys, we rather uncompromisingly called it the "Dead Shop". The nomenclature of the day also called the police station the "Cop Shop".

In reality, is is an obvious term, reflective of ownership and trade. It is true that sweet shop and chip shop, clothes shop and book shop, clearly denote a retail function. Our use of shop was also applied to home. Agreeing a visit to a friend would be supported by the phrase "Your Shop". Derogatory terms, though not meant in harm, such as "spot", "hole" or "pit" are still in common usage as are television influenced words such as "gaff" and "drum".

The derivation of shop can be traced to the identity parade of shop nomenclature a hundred years or so ago. They didn't go by the functional titles of "fancy goods" or "newsagents" or "bakery", instead the name of the proprietor was written in bold with the trade in lesser letters - Whitehead, Gregson, Edmonson, Graham. Thankfully, Appleby still has some distinctions necessary. For example, witness Cairn and Ewbank, our butchers, and Cleator and Bailey, our electrical goods suppliers.

Times change quicker than my typing fingers. In the few months of putting this work together, both Cleator and Bailey's stores are now signless, awaiting inspiration for a new commercial age or more sheckles to fund new notices. Even now modern shop names such as Party Shack fade not through lack of effort but because the competitive marketplace fails their corner.

Thankfully Appleby has yet to step into the shapeless ill-defined world of characterless shops devoted to mobile telephones and sun bed salons, cyber cafes and faceless franchises coloured with livery serving to embrace shallow aesthetic and short-term profiteers.

I digress from the mortuary. I recall seeing my first passing person through a cracked glass pane on the side of the building when I was about ten. Stretched out on a central slab, with labelled toe poking out from under long blanket, it was the stuff of nightmares. A cold, methodical place that gathered stories still to be told from its dry walls and smooth floor. Originally built around the turn of the last century the building operated as a pumping station sending water to the railway stations high above the town. Later, its talents lent themselves to a dairy function milking the chill template offered by clinical walls.

The demise as a mortuary left the building devoid of a function and it was laid to rest. Entrepreneurs capture opportunities when others fail to see them and before long the building was in use again. This time as a bicycle hire and repair shop. It seems that the shop had a mountain to climb and wonderful hills of the locality proved restrictive on the bicycle using population. Trends come and go. Indeed, they are cyclical!

At the time of writing the building was to enter a

new phase of its morphological existence. As a detached place of residence there is no doubting its uniqueness. One can imagine sluice drains previously used for, well, you can guess, being perfect to protect against flood waters. The house with an in built flood alleviation scheme. I doubt if any other building will share such a marvellous location with such an odd history.

The row of newly built houses, Riverside Court, which arrogantly ignore the rules of ascendant house numbering out of town, was previously the site for Burne & Son, the Sands Garage. We knew it simply as Burnes'. Positioned, in its day, on one of the busiest corners of the town as traffic ploughed (sometimes literally) along the A66 - the road to hell and often nicknamed the A666. Burnes' was a Chrysler Dealer, Hillman specialist and Shellubrication Service Station. Like the mortuary, it lay dormant for many years before its metamorphosis into residential property.

The demand for housing strangely contradicts the number of services available to new occupants. The 21st century Appleby is, some would say, going in three directions. A haven of holiday homes, a mobile commuter community who close their doors when they get home, and a stepping stone to heaven for an ever-increasing elderly generation. The disposition of new homes on the fringes of Appleby

will, supposedly, boost the population. No attempt is overtly visible to entice nascent new numbers down the slopes with the wallets to wage the town's retail trade.

Where will Appleby be in the future and how will its social dynamics cope with its demanding visitors and dysfunctional out-workers; without the backbone of loyal old-timers long since lost to the cemetery? I do not want to predict dystopia, I would not be the first if I did. Optimism is the strength of Appleby and its survival instinct contradicts the natural Cumbrian mood of pessimism. I have great hope and faith in the Appleby resilience.

Burnes' Garage, photograph by John T. Hall.

JITTY

My first car was a diarrhoea-coloured mini. My father bought it for me to commute to my first place of work, the MAFF investigation unit at Merrythought, Penrith. One of Thatcher's commuters! Living at Slapestone House in Battlebarrow, we had to rent a home for the car. The barn at the foot of Battlebarrow, opposite Burnes' Garage was available. The vast building could have taken two or three cars so

my Mini was lonely. Cold too, for the walls did not protect it against ice and frost.

Today the car is undoubtedly on a scrap heap in the sky. The barn is not. Carefully renovated it is now Jitty Cottage, appropriately named after the steeply inclined lonnen which runs behind. Such effective modernisation won the property a prestigious Appleby-in-Westmorland Award in 1999, granted for considered care in regeneration. It is hard to imagine but the hard ground behind Jitty Cottage used to house a large iron building used just once a week by Guy Metcalfe as a Sunday newspaper stall.

There are many narrow alleys and passages between streets in Appleby. Most will have their "nick-throughs" whether official or unofficial. Jitty is a common nickname for such a feature, but Appleby has a formal route with the label. The Jitty connects The Sands with Garth Heads Row.[1] Limbs quiver in unsteady unison as graft and gracious gravity are required to secure safe passage along its broken gradient. The midway curve fools the feet and offers little support whether in ascent or descent. It saves the legs

[1] How many of you locals say Garth's Head Row?

of very few users now, as most walkers find it equidistant and easier to use the more substantial path through Lady Garth's above the Sand's Methodist Church or the footpath aside Station Road.

The Jitty also offers a treacherous floor of cobbles, dangerous to heels during all seasons. Take a trip (a safe one) when you can. The cobbles will not be there forever. Men in suits, perhaps those who moved the Butts playground, will surely deign it unsafe, in our litigious age, and assign the Jitty to a tarmac burial. I hope not.

DUCK ISLAND

A popular feature of both parents and children, Duck Island offers a feast of sublime respite after a busy trek around Appleby. With hypoglycaemic young kids screaming for ice-cream or chocolate, distraction is at hand. Whether they are soggy scraps of chips or left-over luncheon crusts, any hint of food will beckon an avalanche of admirers from the town's duck population. Keeping kids and feathered friends happy and excitable, until the scraps run-out, it offers a five-minute seated sojourn for the adults.

The duck population has seemingly exploded over

the last twenty or thirty years, perhaps, in part, due to the increase in people with picnics or, perhaps, there is "something in the water". The population of mallards and moorhens is monitored and controlled as their bravery and bravado knows no bounds in the battle for morsels of comfort. They know which side their bread is buttered; as do the huge gulls, faster, sleeker, larger.

The most popular ducks are a pair of, seemingly, loving Muscovy ducks. Always to be found in the vicinity of Eden Bridge Café they waddle and paddle about as if they own the place. With appropriate appreciation, they go by names common to the area. Not Clifford, nor Pembroke, nor Hothfield, nor Thanet, nor Wharton, nor Whitehead; but "Sowerby and Jones". Sowerby is the largest of the pair and is fun to watch as his chest is pushed out and stumbles follow struts, as Sowerby seemingly knows no rest. Jones, the smaller of the two is more experienced and happy to pant along behind with cheery abandon. Flirting with the curious wanderer, they are obviously fond of each other, but with nothing quite like them around, they have little option.

Duck Island is an ever-changing feature of the river with a personality determined by the discrepancies of the weather. A two-week dry spell, rare as it is, can cause the river to run low prompting grass, weed and bush to sprout across the speckled mound. More common is the rise and fall of the river and the shifting stones of the island. In my lifetime the perimeter of the island has seen a few homes in this stretch of the river. Years ago I remember it being closer to the bridge itself. It was easy to walk behind the middle parapet from the island, itself linked to the "shore" on the shallow Sands side. Today the majority of the island is in line with the red-painted shelter on the town bank previously known as the Vicar's Bank. This is more or less the position seen on the map of Appleby from 1754.

In heavy rain, well-irrigated fells pour water down and the River Eden rises rapidly turning a rich muddy red. Deposits of new stones and sand are laid down as

the island shifts beneath the mighty current. Floods may be alleviated but at some point the banks will break once more as they did in 1983, 1968 and most famously in 1822 (when St. Lawrence's Church was, supposedly, three feet deep in water). In years to come, the water flow will remain in charge and will see Duck Island shift once more. Sowerby and Jones will be long gone and so will you and I.

KING'S HEAD COURT

Appleby's main bridge goes by a number of names, sometimes Appleby Bridge, sometimes Eden Bridge and sometimes St. Lawrence's Bridge. It was built in 1888 and forms a focal viewing point for the river. It remains popular as a picture postcard reminiscence of Appleby but, as I mentioned in the introduction, I want to avoid that side of things. So, take a look at the other side of the bridge. The better view, more with nature at least, is upstream, unspoilt by motor traffic.

In keener days I have canoed down from Jubilee to this point and on to Holme Farm Bridge, but not yet as far as Whirly Lum! I see no reason why those keen days should not resurface, so keep your eyes peeled for my splashing oars. I also have a vision of swimming the route and would welcome companions for such an adventure. Of course, my intentions will need to make the task different (odd at least!) and so I propose it is done, not naked, but on New Years Eve.

On the inner town side is the enclosed area of King's Head Court. Recently revamped to include a small arrangement of retail outlets it has yet to blossom. However, its location should soon attract as the ravages of foot and mouth on tourism subside. Warm and dry weather will help. Perhaps their individual ambition is tempered by squirarchical thumb screws. To improve in wealth many must board the retail merry-go-round.

Grayrigg (then called Gray Ridge on the Appleby-Kendal road) and was responsible for bringing Fox to Firbank for his famous preaching to thousands of Westmorland Seekers in 1652.

Francis Howgill was jailed in his own beloved county for refusing to swear allegiance to King Charles II and fitting, I suppose, that he was incarcerated in Royalist Appleby. I couldn't resist an extended piece of history here as it is not often seen in the guide books, which are usually devoted to the 17th century contre temps of Clifford and Cromwell. My great uncle, Rev. Will Hayes, writes in his biography of Francis Howgill:

The lovely site is steeped in a lively history. St. John the Baptist's Chantry used to sit on the bridge, at least in this vicinity, as the current bridge is relatively new. Reformation suppressed its use and the chapel building became used for the town's gaol, in place of one housed at the castle. The gaol fell into disrepair in 1714 to be condemned much later in 1761. A good example of Appleby's timely decision making! A

Francis Howgill never saw Gray Ridge again with his mortal eyes. He died in Appleby Gaol - his first prison and his last - four years later, i.e. in 1668. These four years were really busy years, as we gather from Howgill's writings. The prisoner made many friends. Even his gaoler became his friend before the end. And the Mayor of Appleby and other persons

house replaced it but this too was lost as the entrance to the new bridge was widened to cope with the increased market traffic, but also to replace the old Norman bridge then considered unsafe.

The gaol saw many prisoners from petty thieves to political activists. More serious criminals would have preferred a custodial sentence against the hanging incurred on Gallows Hill (near Fair Hill). Amongst the political activists held here were the Quakers of the 1660s, notably Francis Howgill and James Nayler, two of the George Fox's Valiant Sixty, and founders of the Quakers Society of Friends. Howgill came from

of note were among his visitors. And from Appleby Francis Howgill sent letters to Quakers. These are preserved in his writings. They are chiefly letters to the persecuted and to the imprisoned. One of the last of them is addressed: "From Appleby Gaol, the place of my rest, where the days and hours are pleasant unto me."[1]

Perhaps it is because of Appleby's Royalist roots that a Meeting House for Quakers was never built in the town. Republican Kirkby Stephen and friendly Kendal both became Quaker towns. Penrith too, with its modern turnpikes of motorway, inter-city line and baseline acceptance of all comers, took in a Quaker House. It could also be that the visiting Quakers failed in supplying the four

Quaker principles to their vision of Appleby. Peace, Simplicity, Equality and Truth have rarely been satisfied as a whole through Appleby's ubiquitous history.

The King's Head looks like it has seen better days and it has. The 1890 guidebook to the town features a full-page advert for the hotel and boasts it is: "The only hotel in the town with hot and cold baths" and proclaims that: "The hotel omnibus awaits the arrival of all trains".

I expect and hope that the hotel will see better days again as Bridge Street begins to, albeit slowly, get itself back in order. Its current array of stores serves the community and tourists alike with the trades and disciplines of today. Estate agents, tea rooms, business services,

[1] Will Hayes, *Gray Ridge - The Book of Francis Howgill*, 1942

lady's fashions, garage, toy shop, sports shop and model shop complete a very busy street. Sadly the equally busy road detracts from a welcoming appearance.

The road is unique as it takes a sharp corner by the Low Cross end into the Market Square (more of that in the next section), but this uniqueness needs something else. I shudder to think of the reaction I would receive if I were to suggest traffic lights, as Appleby must be proud of always being traffic light free. But I will. Bring back the cobbled effect; make the street single

lane with lights in Boroughgate and filter on the Sands, and the welcome becomes more profound. Lady Anne's Pantry could expand to include an outside terrace, Pause For Thought can have an ice-cream kiosk outside, and King's Head Court can enjoy prosperity.

In truth I respect Appleby all the more because it refrains from modern intrusions such as traffic signals, formal crossings and even roundabouts. Anyway, what chance our drivers? Too young and too old, too fast and too slow, they struggle enough with the plain roads as they are.

MARKET SQUARE AND BULL RING

Our journey comes full circle with our final odd corner and the one that has shaped the nature of the town. Through Bridge Street and back into Boroughgate sees the completion of the long loop of string that started at Bankside Books. The odd corner linking the Market Square to Bridge Street is home to a shop awaiting new business. In its many exchanges it was once the tailor, John Brass Cusson's. For many years it was the Toby Jug café and sweet shop run by town stalwarts Vera and Joe Scott serving Mams and Kids until those Kids became Mams; and finally the Eden Chocolate Shop took a turn. Like much of Appleby's vestibules it is now empty awaiting new custodians.

The musical chairs of the town's larger functional commodities will settle in time while stores will continue to change hands. As trade and survival depends more and more on the visitor, the very features of the town that made it an ideal military defence serve to dictate its uneasy commercial fulfilment. W. Douglas Simpson in an address given to the Cumberland and Westmorland Antiquarian and Archaeological Society at Appleby on 1 September 1948 relates the strange geometry to Appleby's contrasting priorities:

On such a site of strong relief, the requirements of defence and commerce come into conflict: the military criterion is difficulty of access, whereas the commercial criterion is smoothness of ground and easy approaches. The military element being dominant in the foundation of Appleby, it was the commercial function of the borough that had to suffer.

The castle was placed on the loftiest part of the terrain, in the manner of an acropolis. The town stretched down into the river loop, with the result that the lower end of its street market, which should have been the main inlet for trade, is hemmed in by the loop of the river. A solution of this dilemma is found in the building of a medieval bridge. But in the burghal lay-out room had also to be found for the parish church and cemetery, and on this constricted site these could be placed nowhere else but in the apex of the loop. No other place indeed could be found if the church and churchyard were not to compete for the valuable frontages on the market street. Out of such complex conditions arose the remarkable right-angled approach from the market place to the town bridge, which is one of the most interesting features in the morphology of Appleby.[1]

[1] W. Douglas Wilson, *Transactions of the Cumberland & Westmorland Antiquarian & Archaeological Society*, 1950.

The Market Square still sees a regular local market on a Saturday and occasionally it is expanded for special events. Stalls parade their wares from the Cloisters at the church to the lowest tree on Boroughgate. Trade can still be brisk but it depends on many uncontrollable factors such as weather and mood. Necessity no longer plays a part and cheese and cattle markets alike are long gone. Even the Saturday market leans strongly towards tourism rather than with fayre for local need.

Appleby has always taken to the uphill struggle in selling its produce. Yet, whether it be from the field or the factory, Appleby continues to be known, famously, as a market town. Today it does depend on tourism and by protecting its past it patents its future. The Market Square once wished to lose its enchanting Moot Hall as it threatened the space required for markets. Now the Moot Hall protects as an heirloom for clicking cameras (and matters of local office). The town remains in mid-league safety, as does its defiant market. Not as busy as Ambleside, not as barren as Alston.

The Moot Hall, standing in the middle of the street, certainly dominates the Market Square and it is difficult to imagine the wide parade without it. Moot is traditionally supposed to derive from "mote" or "mot" meaning an assembly of people or a meeting where transactions of business take place. The adjective moot is originally a legal term dating from the mid-16th century, itself deriving from the noun moot, a hypothetical case argued for the sake of debate. From this we see a *moot question*, a *moot point* and of course, our own Moot Hall - the fitting premises for such discussion and still very much the case today, as it is the site where the Appleby Town Council hold their meetings. Critics would argue that a *moot point* is now formally defined as a case, however debatable, of no practical value and that Moot Hall mirrors this definition. With some irony I would contest in response the fact that its nomenclature opens debate supports its continued existence and profitable worth to the town's heritage.

The lower part of the Moot Hall used to be occupied by open "shambles" and butchering rooms. They now house formal shops and, with particular poignancy, the tourist information centre and exhibition room. The occupiers of the Moot Hall were, and are, very much part of the market trade. St. Lawrence's Fair, also known as the Lammas Fair was held on 21 August, St. Lawrence's Day. Treated as a celebration, the fair of horses, sheep, lambs, cheese and merchandise of great variety was "walked" by the mayor and members of the corporation who visited the Grapes and the Kings Head

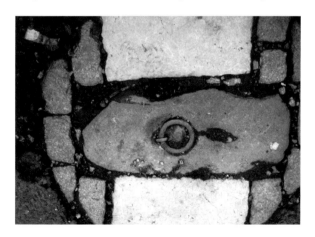

for refreshment. Walking the fairs stopped in 1885 as the importance of such public occasions declined.

Appleby's market and fair traditions are almost too numerous to mention. Garnett in *Westmorland Agriculture 1800-1900* (1912) refers to a new monthly fair for cattle and sheep being held on the first Thursday in each month from January 1835 and then expanding to every alternate Thursday during winter from 1849. Recognising the market as more for "fat animals," the mayor, in 1862, announced that the: "fat cattle market would be changed from the first Thursday to the first Saturday in each month". We still have a Saturday market, but with few fat animals on show. Garnett continues his fascinating insight into the busy trade with precise dates and details of every Appleby fair. For instance, the wool fair beginning in 1837 was held on the last Wednesday in June and July; at the July fair in 1865 about 10,000 fleeces were shown. Market officers were much more in prevalence than today too. It will be a long time since we have had swine-lookers, house-lookers, market-lookers, ale-tasters and clock-keepers on parade on a Saturday morning.

Stuck fast into an irregular stone flag, between the Eden Pharmacy and Flower Basket on one side of the street and the Tufton Arms on the other, is the Bull-Ring. Unmarked and easily missed. Lamely alone as a

threatening nuisance to car-owners alighting blindly into a gathered puddle, even on dry days it seems. As an obstacle befriending no-one, leaving as it does pedestrians loose-footed in the road and market-stall holders frustrated, it maintains a ghostly reminder of harm.

Bull-baiting supposedly continued until 1812. According to Mathews and Whitehead[1] the last bull to be baited was a red roan from Yorkshire with a known reputation for anger. A mastiff dog brought to bait the bull also had a resilient temper and succeeded in clamping its teeth into the bull's nose. With nothing to lose and with all pain muted the bull broke free and ran amok around the town. Coming to rest in Doomgate, the dog was supposedly still clinging tight to the bull's nose. Appleby thus proved to be ahead of the times, for once, as bull-baiting was still carried out elsewhere until an 1835 law prohibited such street events.

Bull-baiting was one of a number of extreme sports enjoyed by the thrill-seeking customers of painful spectacle. Cock-fighting and badger-baiting were also popular pastimes across the north. For sheer scale the

[1] *History of Appleby*, 1950.

bull's demise perhaps brought the biggest crowds. Fastened by the ring in its nose the bull, already doomed to slaughter, would be baited by frenzied dogs and, presumably, by the noise of the jostling crowd. Eventually failed with bloodied exhaustion the slaughtered bull would be placed on sale in the market and labelled, by candles or suchlike, so that the buying public could identify the baited beef, thought to be better in quality for the baiting. It perhaps says something about the humility of the townsfolk that while bull-baiting was stopped in 1812, public executions continued, on Gallows Hill, until 1828 and formal hangings in the gaol carried on until 1840.

Was Palmer correct in his prophecy for the town? Are Appleby's descendants dozy and dim, or are they battling and bidding for a secure middle ground status in order to ensure longevity? Few token gestures contribute to the hard working ethic of the townsfolk whose loftiest goals are gratefully satisfied by simple things. The leitmotif of existence is closer to contentment than frustration of under-achievement. True, there can be cracks in the armour, but there is usually someone to step forward from the ranks.

The strength of the Appleby rank and file is that they are neither front line, nor hiding with a shy guard at the rear. Middle-ground sanity. Palmer's surface view may be correct, not to assign somnolence as this does infer disregard, but to congratulate the town in a simple acceptance of ambitions achieved. Those wanting higher stakes pass through and move on fearing capture in a townscape asylum. Only when they return, and I speak from experience, do they see it as a living Elysium.

Still, the town must retain an alert vision within its tranquil mood if it is not to turn over and go to sleep forever. Much is made of ancient societies who look after their own affairs directed by a circle of elders who dedicate time and experience to protecting the new blood from pollution. Appleby's clubs and committees, primarily its ebullient town council behave like native elders without retiring accelerated decrepity. Indeed, one might believe that they were born that way. I only hope they do not lose interest or fall into narrow-mindedness unable to accept the necessity to nurture the needs of the next generation, and generations as yet unborn.

Defence and commerce still battle on in complex harmony. Defence is now one of resistant attitude rather the protection of territory. It is easy to see that Appleby does take its strength from its past. Whether it stumbles to a halt keeping both feet locked in the time warp or allows itself to move at least one foot forward will determine its prosperity for tomorrow's market place. One thing is clear, Appleby will not be rushing to change its way of life or how it is viewed from outside and from within. The town and its people are unique in giving us that Appleby aesthetic.

Like the earth beneath our feet, the odd corners of Appleby provide the environment that colours the character of the people. Competition for space, physical and hierarchical, combined with a kind compromise confirms that man's only known constant, of change, borders on truancy in the activities of Appleby. The relationship between brick and body fulfils the mantra

of grow slower, live longer. Whether observing creation or erosion, if you live in the town, or are simply passing through, take the time to pause and absorb the spirituality of the place. It will be worth it.

COMMON CORNERS

FRONT DOORS

We have taken a tour of the corners of Appleby that influence the character and personality of the townsfolk. The relationship has come full circle as it is without doubt that it was the colour and wisdom of the townsfolk that designed the corners in the first place. The integration is complete when the home falls into consideration. To be precise, when the access to the home is put under scrutiny. Whether by

choice or design, your door will influence your outward perceptions and lay down the apparel with which you wish to be viewed. Doors are an entry to your territory, your home, your possessions, your comfort. Modern doors tend to lack style and flare, preferring to become slaves to commerce and a fast but inefficient world.

A trip around any city, town, village or hamlet will reveal doors of different sizes, scales and substance. Presented here are just a few doors from the confines of Appleby's centre. Illustrating an imagination and craft, they may also reflect the camber of the person living behind them. I give you no clues as to their location and ownership. Put on your walking shoes and find them for yourselves.

LITTLE ROOMS

There are two basic rules of being a tourist out with the selection of attraction. The first concerns input. If you have the opportunity for food, then eat. The second concerns output. If you have the opportunity to use a toilet, do so.

Appleby has its fair share of public toilets, yet their location has changed over recent years. Travellers alighting at the railway station will be encouraged to find the premises well-served. Although ladies should be warned that their little room is indoors and locked

away out of hours.

The failing Shire Hall may be regenerated to make the adjacent utilities more noticeable to the needy. The most frequently overflowing must be the companion sets in the corridor to the Public Hall, off the Market Square and the large new block, commanding unde-served attention at the rear of the King George V car park.

In my lifetime I remember the rooms of necessity in other locations. The lower end of the Moot Hall used to be home to a gentleman's corner and both sexes were

served by an adequate indentation in the old gasworks wall, by the scout hut, before being deemed inconvenient.

My favourite amenity, and it may be a gentleman's preoccupation to rank them akin to favourite hostelries, has long since been demolished. What irony in this town of preservation that the previously listed building was demolished having "outlived its usefulness" and is now home to a sometime unkempt memorial garden in the name and honour of the town's historian, Martin Holmes. If horticultural support is given to this perfect picnic area by Town Bridge, I believe it would elevate this ailing Appleby angle to respected Odd Corner and inclusion in More Odd Corners should that come about..

EUHEMERISM

For thousands of years we have dreamed of going back. To what, exactly? Eden is a home from which we have been evicted. We stand on the sidewalk on tiptoe and find the window is just a few inches too high to peer in. Exactly what evicted us? History? Society? Sheer numbers? The need for food? The retreat of the glaciers? Adulthood? Birth?[1]

I considered calling this book Old Corners of Appleby. Its timeless traditions would encourage such a title. Appleby has no sinister emotion in its tactical relationship with the past. It does not need to rebuild cobbled courtyards or themed establishments over-fragrant with yesteryear. It does not need to turn its wood and stone into the metal and plastic of the sterile franchise of Anywheretown. Its soul is rooted in its evolution. One step behind or one step ahead of the rest of the World?

The spiritual reference above confirms my choice of Odd over Old. Primarily out of respect for my mentors in the literary world and the travelling philosophers of compact communities. Odd is also an apt description of its peoples and personalities, avenues and architecture, contrasts and cultures of the town. Always on the verge, the corner, of something impressively grand or of something delicately disastrous. I flirt with success and failure in the same manner, but truly believe that if we are to nurture our vision of Eden, we must protect the future by preserving the past.

Gareth Hayes, 2002.

[1] Evan Eisenberg, *The Ecology of Eden*, 1998.

BIBLIOGRAPHY, SOURCES AND RECOMMENDED READING

Along the Pennine Way, J. H. B, Peel, Cassel, 1969

Appleby Castle, Martin Holmes, F. I. H. Ltd, 1974

Appleby Grammar School, Edgar Hinchcliffe, Whitehead, 1974

Appleby Official Guides, 1890, 1962, 1975

Appleby-in-Westmorland and Warcop, Michael Ffinch, Titus Wilson, 1984

Appleby-in-Westmorland, An Historic Town Guide, Barry & Vivien McKay, Barry McKay Rare Books, 2001

Around Eden, F. B. Chancellor, Whitehead, 1954

Eden Benchmarks - Sculptures for Sitting, Dick Capel, East Cumbria Countryside Project, 2002

Eden Valley - Walking Country, Paul Hannon, Hillside, 1996

The Eden Way, Charlie Emmett, Cicerone, 1990

Exploring the Eden Valley, Gordon Wood, Dalesman, 1979

The Geology of the Appleby District, Albert Gilligan, Whitehead, c.1920

A History of Appleby, Martin Holdgate, Whitehead, 1956 (1970 & 1982)

In Search of Westmorland, Charlie Emett, Cicerone, 1985

John Wesley's Journal, Abridged Version, Kelly, 1903

The Parish Churches of Appleby, Martin Holmes

The Pennine Dales, Arthur Raistrick, Methuen, 1968

Penrith and the East Fellside, Michael Ffinch, Hale, 1985

Railways of Cumbria, Peter W. Robinson, Dalesman, 1980

St. Mary's Priory, Appleby, Lancelot H Thwaytes, Barry McKay Rare Books, 2001

Through the Carriage Window, Len Sims and Chris Darmon, Dalesman, 1986

A Tour of Westmorland, Sir Clement Jones, Titus Wilson, 1948

Two Way Guide to the Settle Line, James R Wood, White Frog, 1989

The Upper Eden Valley, G. Gordon Wood, Dalesman, 1968

Walking in the Eden Valley, Harold and Brenda Sowerby, Dalesman, 1979

Walking through Eden, Neil Hanson, Pavilion, 1990

Walks in North Westmorland, Sir Clement Jones, Titus Wilson, 1955

Westmorland, J. E. Marr, Cambridge, 1909

The Westmorland Heritage Walk, Mark Richards and Christopher Wright, Cicerone, 1987

Westmorland Way - Walking Country, Paul Hannon, Hillside, 1983

The Worthies of Westmorland, George Atkinson, Robinson, 1849

All the following books by William T. Palmer F.R.G.S., M.B.O.U., F.S.A.Scot.,

Tramping in Lakeland, Country Life, 1934

Odd Corners in English Lakeland, Skeffington, 1936

More Odd Corners in English Lakeland, Skeffington, 1937

Odd Corners in the Yorkshire Dales, Skeffington, 1937

Verge of Lakeland, Hale, 1938

Wanderings in Lakeland, Skeffington, 1945

Wanderings in the Pennines, Skeffington, 1951

The author, 1964, photograph by John T. Hall

MORE BOOKS FROM HAYLOFT

The Building of Carlisle, The Life and Times of Percy Dalton, City Engineer and Surveyor, 1926-1949, Marie K. Dickens
(£8, ISBN 0 9540711 9 0)

The Herdwick Country Cook Book,
Hugh and Therese Southgate
(Hardback, £19.95, 0 9540711 8 2)
(Paperback, £14.95, 0 9540711 7 4)

A History of Kaber,
Helen McDonald and Christine Dowson,
(£8, ISBN 0 9540711 6 6)

A Dream Come True, the Life and Times of a Lake District National Park Ranger, David Birkett (£5.50, ISBN 0 9540711 5 8)

Gone to Blazes, Life as a Cumbrian Fireman,
David Stubbings (£9.95, ISBN 0 9540711 4 X)

Changing Times, The Millennium Story of Bolton, Barbara Cotton
(£12.50, ISBN 0 9540711 3 1)

Better by Far a Cumberland Hussar, A History of the Westmorland and Cumberland Yeomanry,
Colin Bardgett
(Hardback, £26.95, ISBN 0 9540711 2 3)
(Paperback, £16.95, ISBN 0 9540711 1 5)

Northern Warrior, the Story of Sir Andreas de Harcla,
Adrian Rogan
(£8.95, ISBN 0 9523282 8 3)

A Riot of Thorn & Leaf, Dulcie Matthews
(£7.95, ISBN 0 9540711 0 7)

A Country Doctor, Dr. Isaac Bainbridge,
Dawn Robertson
(£2.25, ISBN 0 9523282 32)

Military Mountaineering, A History of Services Expeditions, 1945-2000,
Retd. SAS Major Bronco Lane
(Hardback, £25.95, ISBN 0 9523282 1 6)
(Paperback, £17.95, ISBN 0 9523282 6 7)

Yows & Cows, A Bit of Westmorland Wit,
Mike Sanderson
(£7.95, ISBN 0 9523282 0 8)

Riding the Stang, Dawn Robertson
(£9.99, ISBN 0 9523282 2 4)

Secrets and Legends of Old Westmorland,
Peter Koronka and Dawn Robertson
(Hardback, £17.95, ISBN 0 9523282 4 0)
(Paperback, £11.95, ISBN 0 9523282 9 1)

The Irish Influence, Migrant Workers in Northern England, Harold Slight
(£4.95, 0 9523282 5 9)

Soldiers and Sherpas, A Taste for Adventure,
Brummie Stokes. (£19.95, 0 9541551 0 6)

North Country Tapestry, Sylvia Mary McCosh
(£10, 0 9518690 0 0)

Between Two Gardens, The Diary of two Border Gardens,
Sylvia Mary McCosh
(£5.95, 0 9008111 7 X)

Dacre Castle, A short history of the Castle and the Dacre Family, E. H. A. Stretton
(£5.50, 0 9518690 1 9)

You can order any of our books by writing to:
Hayloft Publishing, Great Skerrygill,
South Stainmore, Kirkby Stephen,
Cumbria, CA17 4EU, UK.
Please enclose a cheque plus £2 for UK postage and packing.
Tel: +44 (0)17683) 42300
For more information see: www.hayloft.org.uk